TRUST ME, I'M NOT A POLITICIAN

A simple guide to saving democracy

DOROTHY BYRNE

TRUST ME, I'M NOT A POLITICIAN

A simple guide to saving democracy

Published in 2019 by Short Books,
Unit 316, ScreenWorks, 22 Highbury Grove,
London, N5 2ER

10 9 8 7 6 5 4 3 2 1

A CIP catalogue record for this book is
available from the British Library.

ISBN: 978-1-78072-429-4

Cover design by Two Associates

Printed at CPI Group (UK) Ltd, Croydon, CR0 4YY

FSC
www.fsc.org

MIX
Paper from
responsible sources
FSC® C020471

So I've decided that I'm going to save democracy in the UK. I honestly believe I have at least some of the answers. You may think we are in political chaos but I can help get us out of this mess. If politicians just do what I advise, we'll be heading in the right direction.

Democracy cannot thrive without trust. The people must believe in the politicians or the system won't work. Two actions would contribute significantly to winning back trust: senior politicians have got to dare to tell the truth again, and they have to make themselves accountable to the people again. At present they are not doing either of those things sufficiently.

Truth matters. I learned that in my first

philosophy lecture at Manchester University when we were introduced to Plato. Of course Plato wouldn't be allowed in a university today, he'd be no-platformed for so many reasons, not least because he thought women inferior. But Plato believed that the search for truth and the ideal of truth were key to any successful society. And it's because my life as a journalist has been about seeking truth that I ask you to follow my argument. Across Western democracies, we have politicians trying to tell us truth is relative and something they can just define for themselves, without relating it to established facts. Indeed, they have invented a new concept: 'alternative facts'. This is dangerous nonsense. The frontrunner in all this is Donald Trump. Of course, in order to get away with his lies, Trump has to try to undermine the group who hold politicians to account: journalists. So we must be regularly condemned as purveyors of so-called 'fake news'. Well you don't need to be as clever as Plato to realise that fake news cannot exist. If it was fake, it didn't happen so it wasn't news. Sorry Donald.

Imagine what Plato would make of Donald Trump. In fact, let's bring them together. What you might call a meeting of one mind. Obviously I mean Trump's mind because he's told us he's a genius. A stable genius. What should Plato and Donald Trump discuss? Here's one of my favourite lies – Trump has promoted the notion that the sound of wind-mills gives you cancer. I love it. At first you think it's just nonsense, not a lie. But it is a lie and a lie very much of our time because lying about science is rampant among these politicians who think they can just make up facts to suit them. Trump, of course, has form in this area: he supports the ludicrous anti-vaxxer Andrew Wakefield who I first exposed on TV more than twenty years ago. Trump has abandoned any belief in the primacy of truth. If the leader of a democracy no longer believes in the fundamental importance of truth, then that democracy is undermined. That is what has happened in the US and we must not allow it to happen here.

The Brexit referendum has been the catalyst for a significant fall in trust; but the trend has been downwards for some time. The British people have historically had a healthy distrust of politicians. A Gallup survey in 1944 found that only a third of voters thought politicians were motivated by care for their country. Will Moy of Full Fact – an excellent service devoted to fighting bad information and promoting the good – points out, 'We have to remember the public has always had a low view of politicians. Healthy scepticism is normal but cynicism is dangerous and justified cynicism is most dangerous of all. We now have some people in politics who don't think that telling the truth is something they have to be committed to at all.

That destroys belief in politics.'

Prior to Brexit, it was generally quoted that 21 per cent of the British public trusted British politicians. Yes, it really was that high. Bad news: in a recent survey of 2,000 UK voters carried out in August 2019 for Channel Five Television, just nine per cent of people said that politicians were trustworthy. Far more than nine per cent of the UK population think Princess Diana was murdered – 33 per cent. (Just so you know; she wasn't. I carried out a major television investigation and discovered that she died because she got into a car driven by a man under the influence who went too fast and she wasn't wearing a seatbelt. *Quelle surprise.* Prince Philip is off the hook for *that* particular accident.) Meanwhile, the proportion of the British population who believe in aliens from outer space is 36 per cent. So British politicians are less trusted than the existence of little green men. (And little green women. There's a lot of sexism in the world of UFOs.) But if people, including gender neutral and non-binary people, from outer space frighten you, how much more frightened should you be that more than double the number of our citizens believe in Martians than believe in politicians?

How do we help politicians regain public trust? They don't seem to be helping themselves, so they need outside assistance. They have always been pretty rude to each other. Could you imagine your employer allowing you to bray like a donkey at someone who disagrees with you at work? But some scenes in the House of Commons in autumn 2019, as I write this, have been truly shocking. *The Times* Political Editor, Francis Elliott, said that he could not remember, in his twenty-year career, 'hatred being so nakedly expressed'. At Channel Four, I commissioned a programme about internal divisions in the Tory Party over Brexit. Much bleeping of swearwords was necessary to comply with broadcasting regulations. And they were talking about their fellow party members, not Jeremy Corbyn. Internecine warfare in the Labour Party, especially in the row over anti-Semitism, has also been unedifying. It often seems that politicians have lost all respect for each other.

I'm the head of news and current affairs at Channel Four and maybe you wonder why I, a TV journalist, would want to help politicians regain public trust. The first reason is that, contrary to what many might assume, I believe the majority of politicians honestly started out wanting to do good. OK, it's their version of what 'good' is but they do have a public service ethos. As journalist Isabel Hardman put it, 'Most MPs wanted to go into politics to make the world a better place.' The majority could have earned much more elsewhere. That is not because they are more talented than the rest of us, in case that thought even passed through your head, which I accept is unlikely. It's because so many of them come from privileged backgrounds: two of our three recent prime ministers went to Eton, all three went to Oxford. Some would say all three fucked up their country in one way or another. I have to be duly impartial on that one. What I would say is that whatever bad things resulted from what they did, they did not set out to do evil.

But the really important reason I want to help politicians is that, if voters lose trust in politicians, then they can lose trust in democracy. Brexit has exacerbated what was a growing problem: in that same Channel Five survey, 77 per cent of people said their trust in politicians had fallen significantly since the Brexit vote. And 70 per cent of people said they didn't think MPs were honest. Let's pause on that for a moment: the great majority of British voters think that the people whose job it is to look after their interests are, at best, economical with the truth.

We don't need Sherlock Holmes to help us find the causes. In fact, he might be a clue in himself, given that Benedict Cumberbatch has played both the great detective and Dominic Cummings. Here are a few of the Vote Leave messages: we were told the EU was going to ban the British kettle; we were assured the EU was preventing us from protecting polar bears; and if the threat of French kettles and dead furry creatures didn't frighten us sufficiently, we were informed that Turkey, with its population of 76 million, was joining the EU. For those British bulldogs who could not be moved by threats to electrical equipment or wildlife at the North Pole, there was the wonderful promise of £350 million extra for the NHS every week if we left the EU. Imagine if you had honestly believed those claims and now see them widely derided? How would you feel?

But all those flat-white-drinking remainers in Islington needn't feel smug. Their side talked tosh too and even received misleading support from official figures. The Treasury published analysis which said that, 'a vote to leave would represent an immediate and profound shock to our economy', leading to, 'four quarters of negative growth' and pushing up unemployment by around '500,000 within two years'. It also stated that a Canada-style free trade deal with the EU would leave families worse off by £4,300. In their excellent report published this year, 'Doing Democracy Better', Alan Renwick and Michela Palese criticise this as 'a misleading way to present the figures'. Wash that down with your oat milk froth!

Renwick and Palese went on to complain, 'Our argument is that voters deserve to be treated with more respect – by politicians, campaigners, journalists and regulators – than sometimes they have been. Many voters are deeply disillusioned with what they see as the mendacity of politics. They want information that addresses their questions from sources they trust.' I like the way academics use the word 'mendacity', so much nicer than 'lying'. Research by the Electoral Commission found that 52 per cent of respondents did not agree that the campaign had been conducted in a fair and balanced way; only a third thought it was fair. The House of Commons Treasury Select Committee has also stated, 'The public debate is being poorly served by inconsistent, unqualified, and, in some cases, misleading claims and counter-claims. Members of both the "leave" and "remain" camps are making such claims.' If you had assumed that by voting for Brexit, you were automatically going to get Brexit, you would also feel let down. And should you have lived in Sunderland, your sense of betrayal would have been heightened by the inordinate number of London journalists who interviewed you as if you were examples of Neanderthal Man. The pro and anti-Brexit camps have concentrated on discussing how the Referendum vote might have gone differently if politicians had told the truth. I think an even more serious issue is how all these lies and misleading statements undermined belief in our democratic system.

You might think a journalist, a member of a trade with a low reputation, has a bit of a cheek lecturing people about trust. For a particularly egregious example of this, watch James Murdoch's MacTaggart Lecture at the Edinburgh International Television Festival in 2009. He told the audience that it was important to, 'encourage a world of trust' and that newspaper readers were, 'treated with great seriousness and respect'. Let's delight ourselves by remembering how the UK television regulator Ofcom described him just three years later in his role at News Group Newspapers during the hacking scandal. He 'repeatedly fell short of the conduct to be expected of him as a chief executive officer and chairman'. So much for trust and respect. In fact, the British public don't trust newspaper journalists. At the time of the EU referendum, UK newspapers appeared to have been the least trusted in Europe, according to research by the European Broadcasting Union. They surveyed 1,000 members of the public in each of 33 European countries. The UK had by far the least trusted press of any European country in the survey with a net trust score of minus 51. Look it up if you want to know how you get to be minus 51 but I'll just tell you that Holland's press had a plus 44 trust score. (That's one of the really annoying things about Dutch people; they are forever coming out top on stuff like this and they all have really great teeth.)

The good news is that the British people trust television journalism. Overall, figures from Ofcom show that 71 per cent of the British people trust TV News and 75 per cent of people currently rely on television as their main form of news. Various politicians and fanatics deride us as 'the mainstream media'. I wear that description with pride. We are mainstream. People believe us and they watch us; the average British adult watches 99 hours of TV news a year. Can you think of a politician you'd want to watch for 99 hours a year? Even Donald Trump doesn't watch himself that much. Actually, scrub that: he probably does.

Recently I myself was invited to give the MacTaggart lecture, which is a high-profile talk about the future of the British TV industry, presented to its gathered masses at the Edinburgh TV festival; indeed this book is partly based on that lecture and on the annual Cockcroft Rutherford lecture I gave at my alma mater, Manchester University. My MacTaggart caused some public controversy. I presented evidence about the loss of trust in politics and argued that two key reasons for this were that politicians across the Western world were abandoning belief in the primacy of truth and also avoiding presenting themselves for rigorous journalistic interrogation. I also said Boris Johnson was a known liar, pointing to his record of lies, particularly concerning Europe. To me, my comment was just like saying that one should call a spade a spade. But apparently not. It seems that in modern Britain, one should call a spade a horticultural implement. I also criticised Jeremy Corbyn and Theresa May for hiding from proper public scrutiny and said that, were Margaret Thatcher alive, she would call our modern political leaders 'frit' – her word for cowards.

The resulting furore astonished me. As I have a degree in philosophy, affirming the primacy of truth seemed pretty uncontroversial. I was wrong. *The Sun* condemned me in an editorial.

Downing Street issued a statement saying my language was 'inflammatory' (that one seems ironic now). The *Daily Mail* gave over a whole page to Theresa May's communications chief – later the recipient of a gong for helping her to political failure – so he could criticise me. *The Guardian* was kinder and said it was great that someone had spoken out truth and that a new champion had been discovered.

At 67 years of age, I was discovered! As I have known for several decades that I existed, I was bemused. Still, fame at a late age is not to be scoffed at. We old ladies, or even *wee* old ladies, are not proud. Decades of cervical smears destroy all pride. I also received many hundreds of complimentary messages, partly for these comments, but also because I spoke out about the widespread sexual harassment and assault in society and in our industry. In the day after my speech, about a hundred women I hadn't met before embraced me, one in a toilet for goodness sake. If you come from Paisley, you are not used to human touch. But it's good to learn new things late in life.

However, the most extraordinary result was that a significant number of well-known people in television journalism told me privately that it was time that someone spoke the truth; politicians did lie and also failed to put themselves up for in-depth interviews. One presenter of a rival news programme contacted me from his personal email account. (That's generally what a bloke does when he wants to have an affair with you. My knowledge of that fact is not an admission that I have experienced such an honour.) So how many of these outraged journos went public with any comment? Er... Well step up for a ribbon each Robert Peston and Adam Boulton who, following my lecture, said publicly politicians should not withdraw access to outlets which criticised them. I agree; you can't have a democracy without a questioning and critical press. Journalists should not be the pals of politicians. Indeed it's best not to know them at all if you do a job like mine. Almost all politicians have no idea what I look like despite the fact that I have been in my position for a long time. I regard this as a major achievement and my only concern is that being 'discovered' could spoil things.

Each year, I have to attend a party which brings together TV executives and MPs. I bet you're sorry you don't get invited to that one but I am expected to attend. I do my duty and go up to MPs and say, 'Hello, I'm Dorothy Byrne. I'm the head of news and current affairs,' to which they generally reply, 'Hello.' I am struck by the vanity of the fact that they don't introduce themselves! As so many MPs look the same – white, middle aged, usually wearing glasses, and looking sort of sad and lonely – I often can't tell them apart. May I contrast this with my meeting with Nelson

Mandela. Every journalist in TV has a Nelson Mandela story but mine has a point beyond showing off, although showing off is good too. He walked into the room for my interview and said, 'Hello, I'm Nelson.' He was the most famous person in the world and he introduced himself! Hello British MPs, you could learn from that humility. (In real life, Mandela was extremely attractive. We knew, although it had not been publicised, that he had just split up with Winnie. I had similarly just split up with my boyfriend and that also had not been publicised. I thought of asking him out, but didn't dare. How history could have been different! I would definitely have advised against letting that Thabo Mbeki have so much control.)

But, returning to the lack of public support I received from the significant number of journalists when I spoke out about the primacy of truth, you might ask why, as we don't live in Putin's Russia, these people felt they couldn't support me publicly? A number had also given me information to help me write the speeches in the first place but didn't want to be credited. I don't blame them; they were afraid that the limited access they receive to leading politicians could be reduced. And they were right. This year, Boris Johnson became only the second Conservative Party leader in Channel Four's history not to be interviewed by us at the Conservative Party conference.

Here's something you need to know about British politicians. If you criticise them, they may take it out on you. This can have a chilling effect on the degree to which journalists, especially those who depend on politicians for their daily stories, feel they can criticise. There's a phrase you'll be familiar with. 'They don't like it up 'em.' *Newsnight* was refused interviews with all Labour front bench figures after Emma Barnett interviewed Shadow Justice Secretary Richard Bergon at the launch of the European election campaign. He didn't like being accused of lying about some of his previously stated views on anti-Semitism – so the Labour front bench sent *Newsnight* to Coventry. I used to be a teacher, I never permitted my pupils to stop talking to each other. It would have been detention for Labour there. Even when Theresa May was forced out of her job, a perfect opportunity for a senior Labour figure to go on, they wouldn't appear. During a significant part of the 2017 Election campaign, Sky was banned from the Tory bus. They received no briefings, no interviews, and no questions were taken from them at press conferences. *Channel Four News* was banned from the Brexit Party bus at one point. I believe I am the only head of news in the UK who happens also to have been a licensed bus conductress. If I'd gone around behaving like politicians and throwing people off buses, Blackpool Corporation would have sacked me.

What our politicians seemingly fail to realise is that, the more they stage-manage their media appearances, the less likely we are to believe what they say. It is a vicious cycle. Just look at the US, where accusing the elected leader of being a liar hardly prompts controversy at all any more. He is a man so dishonest that, in their annual round-up of political falsehoods, the website factcheck.org created a new title in his honour – 'King of Whoppers'. When I last looked, the *Washington Post* said he had delivered more than 10,000 lies. In the US, there is a frightening loss of belief in democracy, and one has to assume it is not helped by having a liar in charge. According to the 2018 American Institutional Confidence Poll, only a little over half of young people in the US even believe that democracy is always the preferable system of government, whereas a third think non-democratic government could be preferable. This makes a certain sense as only around half of young Americans think democracy serves the people – the other half think democracy serves the elite. British politicians should read those statistics and be warned about the potential effects of loss of confidence in their trade.

Alongside Trump's lies go his attitudes towards women. Bear with me; the two are interrelated. You will remember he was recorded showing off about his modus operandi with women he finds attractive: 'I don't even wait. And when you're a star, they let you do it. You can do anything. Grab them by the pussy. You can do anything.' Trump's mendacity undermines trust in democracy but his repulsive attitudes towards women undermine trust in standards in public life. In the UK, we have a Committee on Standards in Public Life. Who would have thought? You may not be aware that one of its roles is to advise the Prime Minister on ethics. Try to imagine the scene: a civil servant goes up to our current

PM and says, 'A word about morals, sir…' The committee promotes the Seven Principles of Public Life – selflessness, integrity, objectivity, accountability, openness, honesty and leadership. I hope whoever runs it doesn't get paid by results. To these seven principles, I would add, 'Keep your trousers on unless expressly invited to remove them.'

As I write this, Boris Johnson is the subject of allegations about his sexual behaviour, allegations he denies. A leading journalist claimed he had groped her when he was editor of *The Spectator*. He said no such incident ever took place. Why does this claim have such resonance? When I started out in journalism, nobody would have been interested if I had said someone had groped me. Now, women are speaking out and the stories they are telling are perceived as evidence both of moral decay and powerful men's sense of impunity and lack of accountability. Across the Western world, admirable women and men have revealed to us the extraordinary levels of rape, assault and harassment in every industry. There used to be a feminist statement, 'All men are rapists.' It was a statement of political theory, not fact. There are days now when that almost feels like it might be literally true. Recently, I read that a third of female lawyers said they had been sexually harassed at work, one assumes by other lawyers. There is something chilling about the fact that men well-versed in the law should break it. My own industry has an appalling track record. During my 37 years in the British TV industry, there has been no shortage of sexist bastards I can assure you. We are yet to have the public exposure the film industry has had, but we need it. Although I am more a Me sort of person than a Me Too type, I am convinced that until the full truth comes out in every walk of public life, trust is utterly undermined. I want to, for a moment, describe my own experiences – not to moan, but because I think it's representative of a behaviour once glossed over, but now seen as evidence of a rottenness at the heart of our institutions.

I began my career in ITV and from my very first day the overwhelmingly male management made me feel at home. Or to be more accurate, they tried to come home with me. My colleagues took me to the bar and we were joined by a senior manager. As I was standing on the pavement afterwards, this top bloke suddenly appeared beside me and suggested we get in a taxi together. How kind was that? If I hadn't known the way to Chorlton-cum-Hardy and the taxi driver had just arrived from Kabul, that could have been really helpful. As it happened, my mother had taught me to always memorise the way home, so I was able to tell him his services wouldn't be needed. Services of any sort.

Try to picture this happening now at

Channel Four. Let's pretend Channel Four employs lots of working-class people from the North of England – yes, some people still do nurse that fantasy – and imagine a young bloke called Bert from Accrington on his first day. His new young colleagues take him out to the pub and then I turn up and join them, even though I don't work directly with any of them. Bert gets up to leave. I follow him out. Bert stands on Victoria Street to hail a taxi and I sidle up next to him and say, 'Great news Bert, I'm coming home with you.'

On my first day, a female boss had also told me that a director would take me out to teach me the basics of filming and he would sexually assault me, but I wasn't to take it personally because he sexually assaulted all women he worked with. Sure enough, he did assault me – one of the few examples in my career of the promise of a TV boss coming true. His assault was a criminal offence but who could I complain to? I learned early on that as a woman I was on my own. Not all approaches were offensive. Some were merely ludicrous. When I joined the current affairs series, *World in Action*, I was at that point the only woman on the programme, but I needn't have worried about feeling lonely. Again, there was a man with a kind offer. Even though I hardly knew him, one of the journalists suggested we have sex. I realised I would need to use all my diplomatic skills in order not to hurt his feelings, so I said, 'Don't be ridiculous! Of course I won't have sex with you. Do you just ask random women for sex?' And guess what? He did. I asked him what his success rate was and he said, 'One in a hundred, which is pretty good for me.' Looking at him, I thought it was surprisingly high.

I have endured this behaviour over decades. Just before I joined Channel Four, a television producer inveigled his way into my home claiming he needed to speak to me about work and sexually assaulted me. I had to fight him off and genuinely feared I was going to be seriously hurt. After he left, I thought of calling the police but, like many women in my situation, I realised he would deny everything and the police would say I had invited him in. So I was left the victim. But victory was soon to come. In my first weeks at Channel Four, I held an event to introduce myself to production companies. After my talk, I asked for questions and this bloke stood up. With a leer on his face, he said, 'You may not remember me, Dorothy...' Before he could get another word out, I said, 'On the contrary, how could I forget a man who sexually assaulted me in my own home.' Oh the pleasure of it! Of course, he sat down at once and everyone turned and glared at him. He was never seen at Channel Four again. Indeed, I have never heard of him again, although I assure you I did not do him in. So my advice to men would be: you may

37

think of her as your victim tonight but she could be your boss tomorrow. And to men in my industry with a known record of assaults but whose victims have as yet declined to step forward, I say this: you know who you are. And so do I.

I don't think my experiences are untypical. (That said, I would still recommend television journalism to any young woman embarking on a career. In what other line of work, when some bastard annoys you or you hear of some absolute disgrace can you say to yourself, 'I'm going to make a programme exposing that and I will put a stop to it!' And sometimes we even do.) Icons are falling. Sex scandals have even reached our own dear Queen, with Prince Andrew having to deny he had sex with the seventeen-year-old victim of a convicted paedophile. The Jimmy Savile case transformed attitudes. My family are Roman Catholics and their trust in the priesthood has been destroyed by the paedophile scandals in the church. As it happens, I was eleven years old when I first heard that some Christian Brothers were abusing boys at the school down the road from me. That was 56 years ago. I have chortled and been appalled over decades as various popes, monsignors, archbishops and bishops have said they had only just found out about sex abuse. In 2019, Channel Four revealed that Michael Jackson was a serial paedophile rapist. For many of his fans, this information was so shocking that they refused to believe it and we were bombarded with insults.

In a notorious recent case, a man called Carl Beech came forward with an astonishing set of claims of paedophilia and murder against the great and the good. The Metropolitan Police said his information was, 'credible and true'. They were rightly ridiculed when Beech's story fell apart and he was jailed. A politically-correct belief that alleged victims must always be believed was blamed for the police errors. But I think a key cause of their gross mistake was the fact that trust in leading politicians and other major figures in our public life had fallen so low. Even highly-trained police officers thought it perfectly possible that a Tory MP had murdered two boys, an ex-head of MI5 was involved in one of the killings and a former field marshall and a leading Conservative peer were connected to this paedophile group. The case shows that trust is now at rock bottom.

Now let's return for a moment to Plato and those windmills, and what happens in a world where you can no longer trust that the truth is being told. We left Plato and Donald Trump about to have a chat. Imagine they are in ancient Greece, where windmills were a common sight. Plato speaks: 'Truth is the beginning of every good to the gods and of every good to man.' Trump replies: ' Watch out mate. There's a windmill! Put your hands over your ears or you'll catch cancer.'

Now suppose we introduce Plato to a British politician, genuinely clever bloke, whose attitude to truth has transformed and, many would say, perverted politics in this country. Pretty straight kind of guy. Told us Saddam had weapons of mass destruction when all along he'd agreed to the invasion of Iraq to bring about regime change. Know who I mean? Here's his famous contribution to Western philosophical thought: 'I only know what I believe.' Yes, it's Tony Blair. In our little scene, by the windmill, with Donald Trump lying on the ground in terror of the windmill with his hands over his ears, Plato speaks: 'Er, I think you'll find Truth and Belief are two very different concepts. Next!' The lack of truth over the invasion of Iraq was not to be rivalled in British political life until the referendum campaign. You'll be thinking I'm going to introduce Plato to Boris Johnson and Jeremy Corbyn now. But no way either of them would turn up to a lengthy debate that features searching in-depth questioning by a Greek philosopher. They don't even talk to Emily Maitlis, they're definitely not talking to Plato. Maybe Holly Willoughby.

I believe a key reason Theresa May failed so spectacularly is that she didn't hold herself properly accountable to the British people – both in general, and specifically, on the medium British people trust, which is television. Here's what a top BBC executive told me about her: 'There was no point in even trying to interview her. You might as well have interviewed a robot. She said nothing.' Here is what her chief press officer said to us when Theresa May became the first leader of the Conservative Party in living memory to refuse to give either Channel Four or Channel Five an interview during her party's conference: 'What's in it for us?' I'm always suspicious of a man who calls himself 'us'. I didn't care what was in it for him. He was irrelevant. I would just get rid of all these people. Prime ministers, government ministers, they should just have press officers who organise access to the press. Why are we paying for people who try to manipulate debate? Theresa May's lot did her no favours at all as it turned out. And the mob who worked for Cameron were in the forefront of the campaign against Brexit. Another big success for PR men and spin doctors there.

It was Theresa May's duty – and she talked a lot about duty – to be held accountable. It's supposed to be about what's in it for *us*, the voters. And you know what? Jon Snow or Krishnan Guru-Murthy would have given her a fairer hearing than she received from many members of her own party. Most major broadcasters in this country signed a letter of protest about May refusing to do those interviews. Thank you, other broadcasters. You didn't just protest for us; you protested, I know this, on behalf of the British people because British journalists believe in democracy. Indeed I posit that British journalists have more belief and confidence in the British form of democracy than some of the politicians who have abandoned their proper involvement in the system. Mind you, for two years in a row Jeremy Corbyn only came onto *Channel Four News* during the Labour Party conference. I thought, with it being an annual event, he had mistaken his presence for my birthday present. I was wrong. This year he wouldn't give us an interview during the conference. But I still grew older.

Politicians, if you want people to trust you again, start appearing properly on the media people trust. We are really lucky in this country; we have regulated television that is bound to be duly impartial. Be held to account there and you could be seen to be being honest and transparent. So many other Western democracies don't have that. People in other countries are jealous of us. Our politicians should be using it.

It's even more vital to use TV now because of the rubbish spewing out across the internet. A Reuters Institute report last year, which surveyed people across 40 countries, found that only 23 per cent of the public trusted news they found on the internet. A tiny ten per cent trusted social media news – oh, that is around the same percentage who trust our politicians. I say this to politicians: think about the trustworthiness of the company you're keeping. Be seen with people who are trusted. Don't keep bad company. Consider what that photo with Epstein did for Prince Andrew. So many politicians now prefer to bypass television, a trusted medium, in favour of social media, a form of communication on which filth and extremism is spewed out by the second. They think it's great because they can say what they like unchecked. They think it's a clever strategy. Among the reasons they are wrong is that they are only preaching to the converted and not reaching out to all voters.

Boris Johnson has been proclaimed by Downing Street as the first social media PM. On taking office, he recorded a jolly statement – so much more fun than being grilled by Matt Frei or Jon Snow. It reminded me of something and at first I couldn't think what it was. And then it came to me; that great flagbearer for democracy Vladimir Putin, who also likes to talk directly to the nation. Of course, I am only likening Putin and Johnson in terms of their preference for addressing the nation directly. Johnson has only ever been accused of murdering the truth, whereas Putin has been fingered for being connected to actual murders. Also, nobody could accuse Boris Johnson of having had ridiculous plastic surgery.

Just as Trump has dispensed with White

House press conferences, Johnson has not bothered himself with the prime ministerial press conferences of yesteryear. Almost as soon as he entered Downing Street, he was straight out of the door on a dizzying round of photo opportunities. Journalists could rarely get sit-down interviews; they had to catch him as he examined Kinder eggs full of drugs in prison or looked deeply concerned wearing protective medical clothing. To the viewer at home, the Prime Minister looks like he is open (and possibly about to carry out an operation on a small child, which is somewhat disturbing) but there are no opportunities for probing questions. He hasn't (yet) cottoned on to Trump's trick of letting journalists question him briefly as he gets on and off his helicopter – the noise making any intelligent interrogation almost impossible. Johnson's photo ops have not always gone well. At Whipps Cross Hospital in East London, he was confronted by a father furious the press had been brought in as some form of political stunt. Johnson turned to the press and declared, 'There's no press here.' Plato would have had something to say about that statement.

As for his interviews on social media in which he answers questions sent in by the public on Facebook, we have been told they are 'unpasteurised and unmediated'. Of course, they are also unregulated and therefore under no duty to be duly impartial. We do not show these propaganda exercises and nor do any broadcasters of repute. In Johnson's first, the questions were easy and there were no follow-ups. Here's one: 'How would you protect mental health services?' Break your heart Cathy Newman, could you have come up with that? Call yourself a journalist Andrew Neil, could you thought of this toughie? 'What's going to be done to tackle knife crime?' But the most challenging question of all came last:

'Who is your favourite political hero?' He said it was Pericles. Oh you man of the people! You couldn't resist showing off your lovely classical education at Eton and Oxford. What will it be in future? What's your favourite colour? When will you bring world peace? Do you have any personal morality at all? Oops that last one is a real question. Couldn't help myself.

Trump, of course, relies on social media. If you had asked him who his favourite politician was, he would say it was himself. That is in fact true. Asked who his favourite president was, he said Donald Trump.

Some of you are thinking, 'But if politicians do long interviews, they just get interrupted and attacked.' There was a period during which, in my view, some leading television and radio interviewers treated the grilling of a politician as some sort of game. Hours were spent preparing tricks and traps. But you the viewers, the voters, complained to us. You told us you thought it was unfair and unpleasant. I agree. There were times when I myself would shout at the screen or into the radio, 'For God's sake, just let him speak.' I'm not saying it never happens, but it shouldn't happen. It was wrong and it undermined democratic debate in this country. If you see it happen on Channel Four, complain to me. However, that's not why politicians are failing to come on TV now. Victoria Derbyshire: does she remind you of Jeremy Paxman? No. His style of interviewing and hers are quite different. For three years the *Victoria Derbyshire Show* on the BBC investigated a huge range of problems concerning issues covered by the Department of Work and Pensions, including really important problems like universal credit. And in that three-year period not even a junior minister from that department agreed to come on once to answer the points made.

Politicians will go on *News at Ten* where

they can give a short clip and be in control but they want to avoid the hard stuff. They complain about sound-bite politics, but too often they won't talk for longer than a sound-bite. Some of these bites are so short and repeated so endlessly that they become meaningless. 'Brexit means Brexit.' What would Plato have thought of this 'Brexit means Brexit'? It didn't mean Brexit, because Theresa May never obtained Brexit. More recently, we have had 'Do or die', which strikes me as positively dangerous. I am glad it is not the motto of my own employer. I'd be scared to turn up at work.

How useful to public debate is it to keep repeating these phrases?

It's not just that UK politicians won't debate with us – they won't debate with each other. They regularly refuse to come on programmes with their opponents. In the last election, David Cameron wouldn't appear on Channel Four and Sky with Ed Miliband, even though they were the two main rivals. We had to interview them separately. No offence meant to Ed Miliband but he's not exactly scary, is he? I've seen him in the street and small children didn't run away. It is remarkable to me that the Queen met Martin McGuinness but some of our politicians won't meet each other. Prince Charles even agreed to meet Donald Trump. I would love to have filmed that. They wouldn't even have been able to talk about the weather.

The struggle to stage TV debates prompted one of the most ghastly and humiliating experiences of my career. One day I put on my best togs and went along on your behalf as my audience to see the Prime Minister's director of communication in Whitehall. I put the case for Channel Four to stage a TV debate. And this awful man puffed himself up pompously and told me, 'I don't think the best interests of the public would be served by a debate being on Channel Four.' I looked at him and

I thought, 'I have to sit here and beg you and you are a crook!' Because we all knew he was a crook. He was Andy Coulson, later jailed for 18 months for his role in phone hacking. After he refused me, he said, 'Would you like a biscuit?' I declined his biscuit and went out and stood in Whitehall in a rage. I thought, 'I just went to visit the office of the Prime Minister on behalf of a British public service broadcaster and a criminal offered me a biscuit. How did my country sink this low?'

It is notable that Theresa May told Laura Kuenssberg that the one thing she regretted was refusing to take part in TV debates. And she has lots of things she could regret.

As I write this, there are some signs our two biggest political parties are responding more positively to the idea of election debates. The word is that the leader of each thinks the other is so useless, that he believes he is bound to come out better. Whatever the reason, they should do debates and let us be the judge of who comes off worst – or even best! TV plays a vital role in democratic debate during elections. Viewing figures for election debates and interviews are high, as they were for the recent Tory leadership debate. In the Conservative election debates Boris Johnson deigned to join, around five million viewers watched. Television reaches far more of the electorate than any other medium, including newspapers and definitely including politicians on Facebook Live. As I say, that's why we're called 'mainstream'. Just a reminder to politicians: trust in terrestrial TV news, 71 per cent; trust in internet news, 23 per cent; trust in news on social media, 10 per cent; trust in you… well, I don't want to keep rubbing it in.

Now, some of my kinder colleagues told me things like this: 'They don't dare say anything because if they make one slip, it's blown up on social media.' 'They feel they have too much to lose.' 'They don't dare show even a bit of leg.' Hang on a minute. Politicians are genuinely brave people. Every day now when they go to work they risk being abused, attacked or murdered by terrorists or deranged extremists. Yet they're afraid to tell the truth. That's not good enough. Here's the truth about being a politician in the UK now: 'Anyone could just kill me at any time moment.' Jess Phillips said that. She's right. Sadly. So politicians literally risk death and they won't come on TV and talk to Jon Snow. What's the worst he's going to do to you – dazzle you with his tie? Or did some of them mix him up with the other Jon Snow? It is interesting that Boris Johnson has portrayed himself as the Incredible Hulk but he doesn't dare do battle with Emily Maitlis. At the time of writing, he has not done a single *Newsnight* interview.

Journalists can give politicians a hard time but the strange fact is that journalists are far less cynical about politicians than surveys show the public are. In fact, we probably believe them more often that we should. And sometimes that means we journalists are fooled. Do you remember when the government agreed in 2016 to take in 480 unaccompanied child refugees after a campaign by Lord Dubs? I was the poor dupe who immediately commissioned a film in which we would follow those children. Over months and months, in fact for more than a year, I kept harassing the production company about their failure to crack on with the project. I thought they were remiss. They kept saying to me, 'We can't find any.' It turned out they were not to blame at all. By November 2018 just twenty children had come in under that scheme and 220 unaccompanied children were admitted in total. How many times in recent years have journalists who worked for Channel Four told me in absolute indignation that they have discovered that a government announcement of a new sum of money or a new policy was really just the same sum of money or the same policy that had been announced months before? Watch Krishnan Guru-Murthy trying to get our current junior health minister to admit that alleged new money for the NHS was actually cash the health service had previously saved on capital projects. You can see Krishnan's getting a tad peeved as the bloke keeps denying the truth. If these journalists were so cynical, they wouldn't be annoyed and outraged by misleading statements. So please, all politicians, can you just be straight with us?

The government can make it difficult for us to do our jobs properly. A most annoying habit of ministers is to give broadcast interviews before they've released the full details of what they are talking about. Neil Merrick in a recent edition of the National Union of Journalists' magazine, *The Journalist*, cites a good example of this. The then Housing and Communities

Secretary, James Brokenshire, gave early morning TV and radio interviews about plans to cut rough sleeping. The interviews had to be based on what the government itself had told the journalists because the 77-page document containing the actual policy wasn't available until later in the day. The same happened the next day with a green paper on social housing. As Merrick says: 'Ministers could sit back in the knowledge that the message had reached the right places in the way they wished, and any subsequent scrutiny by journalists would not attract much attention.' That should stop.

Conversely, nowadays when things go wrong, some politicians just disappear. When it was revealed that the then Transport Secretary Christopher Grayling had given a ferry contract to a company that had no ferries, he disappeared and his fellow minister Matt Hancock had to answer questions. And then there were the new railway timetables. Where was Christopher

Grayling when they went wrong? Stuck in the lost property office? At times we have to go to ludicrous efforts to get interviews. When Cathy Newman was investigating allegations of sexual harassment against the Lib Dem peer Lord Rennard – allegations he denied – the only way she could get an interview with Nick Clegg, then leader of the Liberal Democrats, was to ring into his LBC programme as 'Cathy from Dulwich' and force him to take her questions live on air. Ed Humpherson of the admirable UK Statistics Authority dissects political statements without fear or favour. He says, 'One of the things politicians could think about is being willing to admit when things have gone wrong. If you want to get people to believe you when you have good news, then they need to get used to you telling the bad news.'

Here's another technique politicians use: 'You have just one question.' Could you imagine Plato saying, 'You have just one question.' You can see a great example of this when Channel Four's Scotland correspondent Ciaran Jenkins interviewed Jeremy Corbyn about Europe. It was a good question, 'Do you honestly believe that Britain will be better off outside the EU?' I just wish I could tell you the answer. Corbyn didn't give one. Here's a tip: if you ever go on *Who Wants to Be a Millionaire*, and get to phone a friend, don't phone Jeremy Corbyn. You could lose a lot of money.

The most daring interview of last year was carried out by Richard Madeley on ITV. He was interviewing the then Defence Secretary Gavin Williamson and Madeley did something every journalist has dreamed of. He terminated the interview when Williamson refused to answer his question. Several times Madeley questioned Williamson about the fact he had told Russia to 'shut up' and 'go away' over the Skripal poisoning, and several times, Williamson made some other point rather than answer. He even tried to answer by expressing his support for British nurses. Eventually, Madeley said, 'Interview terminated because you won't answer the question [...] It would be helpful if you answered a straight question with a straight answer.' The interview took place in a Midlands safari park and if you watch it online, you will notice that even a passing elephant turned away from Williamson.

I thought of that interview when we heard how Williamson was grilled over the security leak about Huawei. I imagined secret people trying to get the truth out of him and Williamson saying, 'I must insist on stating my very strong support for the nurses of this country.'

The pooled interview, in which one journalist interviews a politician on behalf of all broadcasters, is also overused. Shadow Secretary of State for Exiting the EU Keir Starmer often offers only pooled interviews. That isn't proper scrutiny. One journalist can't ask questions for all journalists; the whole point is supposed to be the diversity of questioning. Press conferences, even when held, can be misleading. Here's what a top BBC person told me about quite a few press conferences you see: 'Press conferences look real. The politician is on one side and the journalists are on the other but the chance of a question which is not pre-arranged being taken out of the blue by a journalist sitting there is very low.' What's scary here is that this could be Russia we are talking about. The disturbing point is that it looks like the way it used to be, but it isn't. It's a visual lie.

Many of you will have seen the excellent recent BBC series on Margaret Thatcher, *Thatcher: A Very British Revolution.* One striking feature was the number of lengthy television interviews Thatcher did. Leaders of the past subjected themselves to half-hour or forty-five minute interviews with the likes of

Brian Walden and Robin Day and held regular press conferences. During the 1987 election, Thatcher and Kinnock chaired daily press conferences and gave several full-length interviews. Even more recently, Miliband and Cameron also did extensive interviews in election campaigns. However, Theresa May, when she was leader, and Jeremy Corbyn failed to hold themselves to account in the same way. In the 2017 election, May and Corbyn did only one or two events a day. During the whole European election campaign in 2019, neither May nor Corbyn did a substantial interview with any broadcaster. They didn't even do interviews on the night of the results. I know those results were embarrassing for them – but so what? Outside of election periods, and setting aside some interviews with Andrew Marr, Theresa May's PR people generally said she would do interviews of only four minutes, maybe six if you were lucky. Throughout her time as PM,

May's longest interview with *Channel Four News* was seven minutes. How do you delve into the complex problems of our times in a few minutes?

For weeks and weeks of the Conservative leadership election, Boris Johnson was virtually invisible on television. The public was able to view him mainly on hustings organised by his own party. Our experience at Channel Four was typical. He kept promising to come onto *Channel Four News*. He never did. He didn't do an interview with *ITV News* or *Channel Five News* either. And he failed to turn up to Channel Four's leaders' debate. We left his podium empty during the debate just in case he changed his mind and popped by. He didn't. Throughout that campaign, Boris Johnson was castigated widely for failing to be held accountable on television. He did the minimum he could – just two leaders' debates, one interview with Laura Kuenssberg and one grilling by Andrew Neil. Once in office, it was several weeks before he did any significant television interviews.

Older politicians are appalled by what's going on. As Ken Clarke said on Krishnan Guru-Murthy's podcast, *Ways to Change the World*, under Thatcher and Major, senior politicians were expected to go out and justify their policies at length. 'Part of the job, I always thought.' He was right. In his valedictory radio programme, John Humphrys asked Tony Blair what he thought of Boris Johnson's failure to come onto *Today*. Blair said, 'When I first began as a politician, your ambition was to get on the *Today* programme. It probably means that he is anxious about a sustained and forensic analysis of what he's trying to do.'

To Humphrys' chagrin, he didn't get a single interview with Boris Johnson as Prime Minister and he didn't interview Labour leader Jeremy Corbyn in the last three years he was in the *Today* chair. Corbyn finally went onto the *Today* programme only after Humphrys had left. I wonder why. Corbyn is rarely to be heard in any significant television or radio interview. Before the proroguing of parliament, John McDonnell said he was going to put Corbyn in a taxi and send him off to see the Queen. That befuddled me as I've been able to get in taxis by myself since I was about twelve. I had the wild idea of sending the Queen – a fellow old lady after all – a camera so that if she was lucky enough to meet Mr Corbyn she could ask him some questions on behalf of the British people, because few of us get to do that.

Corbyn, who began his career on the *Newport and Market Drayton Advertiser* and is even a member of the National Union of Journalists, gave the Alternative MacTaggart Lecture at the Edinburgh Television Festival last year. He said, 'At their best, journalists challenge unaccountable power and expose things that the rich and powerful would rather keep hidden from the rest of us.' Yes, Jeremy but first we need the chance to question the rich and powerful. He also said that, 'fearless journalists and those who support them in their work are some of the heroes of our time.' Go on Jeremy, be a hero, come on *Channel Four News*, or *Newsnight*. You can do it. You can even get in a taxi by yourself and do it. It's easy. You just hail them on the street and they stop. Although, maybe not if you're Jeremy Corbyn. Could that have been the problem?

Meanwhile, Dominic Cummings, allegedly the most important political figure in this country at present, has never done a television interview as far as I can establish. And indeed he has such respect for our democratic system that he was held to be in contempt of it when he refused to appear in front of the parliamentary committee investigating fake news.

You'll hear politicians say you should trust

the voter, not us. And, of course, the voter is the person we ultimately trust in a democracy. But that is quite different to expecting voters to work out which politician is telling the truth. At Channel Four, we gave a representative sample of 1,700 people six news stories – three of which were true and three false. Only four per cent of people identified them correctly. That's not surprising, the public isn't in a position to investigate the truth or otherwise of stories. That's our central job. Journalists are loathe to use the 'L' word but I think we need to tell viewers when someone is not telling the truth. Remember when Andrew Marr told Penny Mordaunt her claim that the UK couldn't stop Turkey from joining the EU was 'strange'? It was strange but it was also untrue, a lie. In fact, accession of a candidate state has to be approved unanimously by the council of the EU which is made up of representatives from each member state.

Boris Johnson's interesting relationship with the truth has been well documented by good journalism. He has lied about the EU for decades. In 1991, he told us that EU bureaucrats rejected Italian demands for smaller condoms. Rubbish. We were told the EU had set rules on the shape of bananas. Nonsense. He said that Brussels bureaucrats had demanded that each kipper be accompanied by a plastic ice pillow. That was simply untrue. Even Donald Trump's never lied about a kipper. More recently, he claimed he was resigning from Theresa May's government partly because the EU had prevented the UK from passing a law to save the lives of female cyclists. What a feminist that man is! So many women say that to me.

Chancellor of the Duchy of Lancaster Michael Gove has implied that we, the media, are the liars, not the politicians. He has launched a rapid rebuttal unit to give instant responses to 'media myths and half-truths' to ensure that we the people 'are not being alarmed by scare stories or falsehoods'. I don't like to be a snitch, but Gove would be well advised to keep an eye on Dominic Cummings, the government's key Brexit advisor and the man behind the kettle and polar bear scares.

There is a more dangerous line which some politicians are taking towards journalists who want to question them critically. When Nigel Farage didn't like Andrew Marr asking him questions about the little issue of his previous support for the relaxation of the law on hand guns, Farage said afterwards, 'The BBC are now the enemy.' The enemy of whom? Well they are not the enemy of the people of Britain because the BBC is in fact massively trusted by British people – 71 per cent of them, according to an Ofcom survey this year. And you know all you had to do, Nigel, was answer his questions. Asking you a question doesn't make a man your enemy. And we're not your enemies, we are the friends of democracy. A ploy of both Trump and some of our own politicians is to accuse journalists of being negative and unpatriotic. Trump regularly attacks journalists for being 'the enemy of the people' and criticises his opponents as negative and lacking patriotism. He even said that the congresswomen he'd wanted to send home should be 'more positive' and reminded them that they had an obligation to love their country. Presumably before they got thrown out of it. Some of you might remember the night that current Secretary of State for Business, Andrea Leadsom, told Emily Maitlis on *Newsnight* that broadcasters should be 'a bit patriotic' because 'we all need to pull together'. Boris Johnson's equivalent of Trump's attack on the negativity of journalists and opponents is to rail against 'the doubters, the doomsters' and 'the gloomsters'. I don't need any politician to tell me to be patriotic. And it's not being a gloomster to question policies. It's the role of the free press in a democracy.

Without free journalism, you can't have democracy. Politicians should be supporting good journalism, not attacking us. If trust is to be rebuilt in politics it is very important that politicians stop slagging off journalists who are doing their jobs properly and start supporting journalism. We journalists need to be sticking up for ourselves more. As well as my Channel Four day job, I'm the chair of an international charity, the Ethical Journalism Network, which supports journalists around the world who are trying to uphold good standards in sometimes very difficult circumstances. History shows that when you want to undermine democracy, the first thing you have to do is undermine journalism. For Hitler, convincing the German people that journalists were liars was key. Whenever some evil regime wants to start murdering people, they start with murdering the journalists or imprisoning them or intimidating them. Criticise us when we get something wrong, don't attack us for doing our job. We are flawed, and need to be more upfront when we make mistakes ourselves, but without a free press, you can't have a democratic free society.

In the difficult period we are entering, we need the truth and we need proper scrutiny of all our major politicians. Television is a bulwark of our democracy, and those who undermine its role are undermining democracy. I have a five-point proposal for British politicians which I believe will help win back trust:

1. Put yourselves up for in-depth interviews.

2. Use the most trusted form of mass media in the UK: television.

3. Give us time to check what you say.

4. Be prepared to debate each other.

5. When you get it wrong, don't run away.

It is time for the television industry to stand up for itself and speak out publicly against what is happening. Yes, we are rivals but we have to form a united front in opposing attempts to sideline our central role in the political life of this country. However, we should get our own houses in order. There's a lot of nobbling and lobbying going on in journalism and we shouldn't have anything to do with it. Particular politicians and special interest groups shouldn't be allowed too much access. I was contacted a few years back by a Conservative peer. He told me that he and a group of his 'friends' had regular dinners with the head of BBC News and several of his top news executives. I asked him who he and his friends were, what group did he represent. He explained they were not a formal organisation but a group of people concerned that there should be fair coverage of Israel.

They had got together because they were angry about some of UK TV's reporting of Israel and they'd like to meet me and tell me their views. I immediately told him I couldn't spend my time meeting groups of men and their friends. Where would it end? I'd be out every night with men and their friends. So, I wouldn't be meeting him. Also, unlike the BBC, I didn't have lots of executives. There was only me and I was a single parent so I didn't have time to meet him. He was really not happy. He complained to my boss and I was told to get back to him.

So I did. I said I'd thought about it very seriously and I had to make decision. Would I meet him and his friends, whoever they were, or would I meet my own child? And I'd decided to meet my child. He said this outcome did not make him at all happy. I said, in contrast, I was very happy indeed. But a few months later I got back in touch with him. I said he maybe thought I'd ignored his approach to me but *au contraire*. As a direct result of our contact I'd commissioned a *Dispatches* programme which was about to be broadcast. Presented by Peter Oborne of the *Daily Mail*, it was called 'Inside Britain's Israel Lobby' and I wanted to thank him for the idea because if he'd never got in touch, I'd never have commissioned the programme. That's what TV executives should do when people try to lobby them. Expose them. Voters don't get that special access and we are supposed to represent their interests, not those of politicians. How can we be equally fair to everyone, if we meet and speak to just the few? BBC journalists I know are always complaining about it, but they make what I regard as the mistake of meeting lobbyists when, in my view, there are perfectly good procedures for people to make their case and a regulatory framework to deal with complaints.

We in the TV industry should also be

more ambitious and make programmes which explore complex ideas about modern Britain. I may criticise some men of the past in TV for their sexist attitudes but they also believed TV was there to say and do big things. They were radical alternative thinkers who believed programmes could be used to make our country a better place. How many people in TV today would say out loud that they wanted to use TV to make Britain a better place? The achievements of that generation were immense – extraordinary investigations like *The Birmingham Six*, great documentaries like *Seven Up* and *Inside the Communist Party*, landmark series like *End of Empire*, a new way of covering elections in *The Granada 500*.

Our country is undergoing seismic changes. There is widespread disillusion and a loss of a sense of belonging. On the news, we're hearing every day that the very fabric of our democratic system is being ripped to shreds. Whatever happens with Brexit, we need big new ideas to take us forward. But too few programmes are analysing that crisis and shaking our assumptions about society. So often I'm told that documentary formats now deal with important subject matters but these formats only describe society as it is, they don't provide a vision for change.

Television is desperate for young audiences. Millions of young people are now politically aware and active. They're prepared to spend hours listening to extraordinarily serious podcasts, often authored by some pretty heavy-duty thinkers. They are out on the streets in massive demonstrations against climate change, searching for alternative ways of seeing the world and for answers to major issues like the viability of our current financial systems. A great TED talk gets millions of views. We have to stop being afraid of serious analysis authored by big brainy people. TV producers scoff at the limited vision of culture which Kenneth Clarke presented in *Civilisation* back in 1969, complaining he was pale, male and stale. But he had a great vision and that series transformed the understanding of art of millions of people, including me. I know that older white men have been over-represented in society, but I am opposed to attempts to drive them out. If they have great things to say, let's hear them. Terrestrial television executives are obsessed by the fall in audiences and forever looking over their shoulders at Netflix and other streaming services, hypnotised by their success. But terrestrial TV still accounts for 69 per cent of all TV viewing, according to very recent Ofcom figures. Terrestrial TV is the only form of UK television interested in saying big things about Britain. That's not the role of Netflix or other streaming services, terrific as they are in many ways. I counted 29 different programmes on Netflix about drugs. I wonder if there's a drug cartel anywhere that's not currently being followed by a streaming service. There's also a plethora of programmes about serial killers. Programmes about mass murdering drug lords will contribute nothing to the reinvention of the UK's political landscape. But when we do major investigations here in Britain, like *Channel Four News*' investigation alongside that of Carole Cadwalladr into Cambridge Analytica, they gain huge traction. The public appetite is there.

Now, painful as it is to admit it, Rupert Murdoch made a very good point in his MacTaggart lecture back in 1989, the very period when I was working on *World in Action*. He said television was 'controlled by like-minded people' who thought they 'knew what was good for us' and criticised TV for reflecting the values of a 'narrow elite'. My vision of empowered and daring producers and commissioning editors who want to shape society for the better doesn't work if all those empowered people are just a bunch of posh boys. By what right do we showcase big ideas if we are such a small group? That matters because we can't reflect society properly if we ourselves don't reflect society. When you change who is making TV, you change TV.

I am proud that I was part of a group of women who changed television. The first report I produced and directed for *World in Action* was about rape in marriage, then not a crime, and two very senior journalists told me it wasn't a suitable subject for the programme and indeed not even a 'story'. They were right. It was more than a story. It was a scandal which besmirched our society. These women-focused shows rated well with audiences but I could tell that quite a few of my colleagues didn't rate them much. My reputation was nearly destroyed when Mary Whitehouse rang up to say how good one of my films had been.

By great good fortune, I took the call. I'm ashamed to say I told her Dorothy Byrne was out but I'd pass on the compliment. I never told my colleagues she'd rung.

The lack of people from ethnic minorities when I started out working for ITV at Granada Television was appalling. I was the equality officer when the main union representing television workers asked us to do a survey of the number of black people working there. I didn't need to do a survey, I personally knew all five black people – out of a workforce of around 1,600. When I reported this back to the joint union committee, one of the 'brothers' said, 'That's five too many.' And another chipped in, à la Trump, that they should all go back home. Of course, I pointed out that this almost certainly was their home. While that would never happen now, the lack of progress in increasing ethnic diversity in television is the single most disappointing failure during my career. I looked at the two reports by Directors UK which came out in September 2018. OK, the figures are not completely up-to-date but only 2.2 per cent of directors came from black and ethnic minority backgrounds. Yes, 2.2 per cent.

There is a specific area where journalists need to sharpen up their act. While a key reason we are trusted is that we are required by regulation to be duly impartial, some journalists have missed that little word, 'duly'. We don't have to be impartial between truth and lies. In fact, our key job is, on your behalf, to tell the truth from the lies. Here's what a former senior BBC news executive said to me: 'People with opinions and arguments have used the idea of impartiality to undermine the importance of accuracy.' In the Referendum campaign, as I have already said, both sides talked tosh sometimes and they were sometimes allowed to get away with their tosh because some journalists thought it was their job to report tosh, not to expose it.

In our political editor Gary Gibbon's excellent small book about the Referendum campaign, *Breaking Point*, he writes, 'One broadcast journalist told me how his bulletins were strictly, almost to the second, timed so each campaign's interview clips achieved perfect balance in each report. The bosses no doubt thought they were rigorously implementing impartiality but they were ducking their duties, abdicating in favour of a stopwatch.' Sometimes the fear about being perceived to be partial means TV apparatchiks end up dancing on pinheads, as when the ludicrously-titled BBC Executive Complaints Unit ruled against the talented Naga Munchetty for calling out Trump's racism.

The obsession with impartiality is even more dangerous when it comes to science. When I worked at Granada, even although we knew smoking caused cancer, when we did a smoking story, we'd be told to get some bloke on saying it didn't. That sort of bad science reporting has continued, in particular with MMR and, of course, climate change. I've made three films in total about the awful Andrew Wakefield, each one exposing him, starting in the late 1990s. But others have given this dreadful man space. *Panorama*, great as it is as a programme, broadcast a film back in 2002 with special access to Andrew Wakefield at work and home. Here's what the BBC publicity said: 'As parents continue to shun the controversial triple jab, despite mounting fears of a measles epidemic, *Panorama* asks how safe is MMR?' Even then, we knew the answer: really safe. You didn't need to make that programme. Seventeen years on from programmes like that, we've got a quarter of a million teenagers who didn't get the MMR vaccine. *Panorama* shouldn't have been at home with Andrew Wakefield, they should have been exposing him, as we did, so that he got struck off as a doctor. We must not report drivel.

Just a few months ago, I heard John Humphrys say on Radio Four that everyone had finally accepted climate change is happening. Hello John, most of us accepted that a long time ago. You know how the BBC found out? David Attenborough told them. Imagine Galileo came along today and said that, contrary to what had been believed previously, the earth goes round the sun. Can you picture how the *Today* programme would cover it. They'd need to get an opposing viewpoint. The editor would demand, 'Get Nigel Lawson on.' Some innocent researcher would say, 'But Nigel Lawson isn't a scientist. How about that Brian Cox? Can't we get him?' The editor scoffs. 'He's an astronomer, he'll just agree with Galileo. The whole point is to have someone who says the opposite – and if he's a Tory grandee, double whammy for the BBC.'

As millions round the world protest over climate change, our top priority as journalists should be telling the truth about science. Journalists have failed just as politicians have failed. The BBC should get Greta Thunberg as one of their *Today* guest editors.

I started my journalistic career on a local paper in East London, the *Waltham Forest Guardian*. It was a paper of nearly 100 pages. We covered every major council meeting and all the planning meetings. Local papers have been decimated by the internet. Without local journalism, you can't have a properly functioning local democracy. This is a democratic crisis. Now, local councils and politicians are reporting on themselves. Joe Mitchell, co-ordinator of Democracy Club, an organisation with 10,000 volunteers devoted to improving our democracy, points out that the most common questions googled in a general election are about who the local candidates are and where polling booths can be found. Local papers used to give people that information as well as describing and questioning the constituency candidates' policies.

Nationally, the new challenges to democracy are frightening. Investigations by *Channel Four News*, *The Observer* and other news organisations have exposed ways in which news on social platforms is used by those outside the UK to attempt to influence voting. This is the new frontline of democracy, with elections potentially influenced by unseen hands. It has never been more essential that politicians should use trusted media. Our democratic systems need to be strengthened to deal with this threat. As Carole Cadwalladr says in her excellent TED Talk on the subject, 'we are what happens to a western democracy when a hundred years of electoral laws are disrupted by technology.' Across Europe in the 2019 EU election, Russian disinformation websites and social media accounts linked to Russia and far-right groups were found to have spread disinformation. Researchers have identified tactics and fingerprints similar to those seen in the 2016 US elections. Here's a scary statement from Daniel Jones from Advance Democracy, a former FBI analyst and senate investigator, about what the external enemies of our democracies are up to: 'The goal here is bigger than one election. It is to constantly divide, increase distrust and undermine our faith in institutions and democracy itself.'

We will need to develop legislation and new structures to protect our democracy from external threats. Journalistic investigation will play an important role, but the threat to our democracy from lack of honesty and accountability must be addressed by politicians as well as journalists for our trust to be regained.

There is a group whose reputation politicians should study. Since 1983, Ipsos MORI has carried out an annual Veracity Index. This was the source of the statistic that only 21 per cent of British people had trust in politicians before our current political chaos. In the same survey, civil servants scored 59 per cent. They are the biggest risers in the table – trust in them has gone up by a whopping 37 per cent in the 35 years since the survey began. Trust in scientists has also gone up hugely – by 22 per cent. Nurses are currently the most trusted profession – 96 per cent. So there are people the public respects more and more – as it trusts politicians less and less. Something strikes me. These people are the 'experts' we have heard some politicians deride. However, as Ed Humpherson of the National Statistics Authority puts it, 'These are professions where people think they put the public interest above their own interests.' Politicians, please note. If you want us to respect you, demonstrate that you respect and care about our interests before your own.

We are at a crossroads. Did politicians enter

Parliament to be despised and disbelieved, or do they want us to admire and respect them as our leaders? Do they want to be likened to Donald Trump or to Winston Churchill?

ACKNOWLEDGEMENTS

I am very grateful to Aurea Carpenter and Helena Sutcliffe for suggesting that I write this book, which is based on two lectures I gave in 2019.

I would like to thank Vice Chancellor Dame Nancy Rothwell and the team at Manchester University who invited me to give the Cockcroft Rutherford Lecture. I also thank Lisa Campbell, Kelly Webb-Lamb and Graham Stuart of the Edinburgh International Television Festival for the invitation to give the MacTaggart Lecture and the excellent lecture producers Yusuf Ally and Camilla Lewis. Diana Aurisch supported me brilliantly in both ventures. Thank you to Ian Katz, my boss at Channel Four, for his forbearance during the row my MacTaggart caused. And for all their help and encouragement throughout, I thank Hettie Byrne, Brad White and Johann Hari.